CONSPIRACIES AND COVER-UPS

FACT OR FICTION?

VOLUME 2

Compiled and edited by
Tom Lyons

CONSPIRACIES AND COVER-UPS: FACT OR FICTION? VOLUME 2

Copyright © 2024 Tom Lyons

All rights reserved. No part of this may be reproduced without the author's prior consent, except for brief quotes used in reviews.

All information and opinions expressed in *Conspiracies and Cover-Ups: Fact or Fiction? Volume 2* are based on information provided by others. Tom Lyons does not purport that the information presented in this book is accurate knowledge.

Acknowledgments

Thank you to those who were brave enough to publicize the following information.

Some of the following names were altered to protect people's privacy.

Would you like to see your report in an issue of *Conspiracies and Cover-Ups?*

If so, all you have to do is type up a summary of your experience and email it to Tom Lyons at:

Living.Among.Bigfoot@gmail.com

Special Offer

If you submit a report and it is accepted, you will receive an exclusive paperback copy signed by Tom shortly after the book is released. If you'd like to participate in that offer, please include your mailing address in the email.

Contents

The Dyatlov Pass Incident 1

The Loch Ness Monster 15

The Oak Island Treasure 30

The Ghost Ship of the Atlantic 44

The Tunguska Event 59

The Lost Colony 76

The Phoenix Lights 92

Conclusion 111

Editor's Note 113

Mailing List Sign-Up Form 115

Social Media 117

About the Editor 119

Conspiracies and Cover-Ups: Fact or Fiction?
Volume 2

The Dyatlov Pass Incident

In January 1959, a group of ten experienced hikers, mostly students from the Ural Polytechnic Institute, set out on an ambitious winter trek through the Ural Mountains in the Soviet Union. Led by Igor Dyatlov, a 23-year-old engineering student and seasoned outdoorsman, the group aimed to reach the remote Otorten Mountain, a challenging route classified as Category III, the most difficult. The hikers were well-prepared for the journey, carrying enough food, equipment, and clothing to survive the harsh conditions. Despite the freezing temperatures and deep snow, they were in high spirits, eager to conquer the treacherous terrain. But the expedition would soon take a tragic and mysterious turn, leading to one of the most baffling unsolved mysteries of the 20th century.

After setting out from the small settlement of Vizhai on January 27, the group made steady progress through the snow-covered mountains.

On January 31, they reached the edge of a highland area near Kholat Syakhl, a mountain whose name ominously translates to "Dead Mountain" in the local Mansi language. The group set up camp on a slope, intending to cross the pass the next day and continue their journey.

But they would never make it. On February 1, something went terribly wrong, and the hikers' journey ended in tragedy. When they failed to return as scheduled, a search party was sent out, leading to a discovery that would haunt the investigators and spark decades of speculation and debate. When searchers finally located the group's campsite on February 26, they were met with a scene that defied explanation. The tent, which had been carefully set up on the slope, was found abandoned and badly damaged. The most unsettling detail was that the tent had been cut open from the inside, as if the hikers had fled in a state of panic. Even more disturbing was the fact that all their belongings, including warm clothing, boots, and equipment, were left behind.

Footprints in the snow led the searchers down the slope, where they found the first two bodies, those of Yuri Doroshenko and Georgy Krivonischenko, lying near the edge of the forest, under a large cedar tree. Both men were dressed only in their underwear and had no shoes, despite the freezing temperatures. Nearby, the remnants of a small fire were found, suggesting they had tried to stay warm before succumbing to the cold.

Further into the forest, three more bodies were discovered, including that of Igor Dyatlov himself. These hikers seemed to have been attempting to return to the tent, but they too had perished from hypothermia. Like the others, they were inadequately dressed for the harsh conditions, wearing only partial clothing. It would take two more months before the remaining four hikers were found, buried under several meters of snow in a ravine further into the forest. The discovery of these bodies only deepened the mystery, as they bore signs of severe, inexplicable injuries. One had a fractured skull, another had broken ribs, and a third was missing her tongue and eyes. Despite the violence of these injuries, there were no external wounds to explain them, and no signs of a struggle. The lack of obvious external trauma, the bizarre behavior of the hikers, and the strange circumstances of their deaths puzzled investigators and led to more questions than answers.

The Soviet authorities launched an official investigation into the Dyatlov Pass incident, but the findings were inconclusive. The final report stated that the hikers had died due to a "compelling natural force," but offered no explanation as to what that force might have been. With so little evidence to go on, speculation ran rampant, and a host of theories emerged, each trying to explain the bizarre events that led to the deaths of the nine hikers.

One of the most widely accepted theories is that an avalanche forced the hikers to flee their tent in the middle of the night. Terrified of being buried under tons of snow, they cut their way out of the tent and ran downhill in a desperate attempt to reach safety. However, the area where the tent was found showed no clear signs of an avalanche, and the injuries sustained by some of the hikers were inconsistent with this scenario.

Another theory suggests that the group encountered a natural phenomenon known as a "katabatic wind"—a powerful, sudden down-slope wind that can create extreme and dangerous conditions. The wind could have caused the tent to collapse, forcing the hikers to flee. But this theory also fails to account for the unusual injuries and the strange behavior of the group.

Some believe that the hikers were victims of a secret military experiment. The Ural Mountains were known to be a testing ground for Soviet weapons, and there were reports of strange lights in the sky on the night of the incident—possibly flares or missile tests. This theory suggests that the hikers accidentally stumbled upon a covert operation and were either killed by the military or by some experimental weapon. However, there is no concrete evidence to support this, and the idea remains speculative. The more paranormal theories include encounters with extraterrestrials or cryptids, such as the Yeti. These ideas have been fueled by the strange injuries, the missing tongue and eyes, and the mysterious orange skin and gray hair of some of the victims, which were reported by some sources but later disputed.

One of the most perplexing aspects of the Dyatlov Pass incident was the discovery of trace amounts of radiation on the clothing of some of the victims. This finding led to wild speculation that the hikers had been exposed to some kind of radioactive material, either through a military test, a natural source, or even an encounter with a UFO.

The presence of radiation has been one of the most controversial pieces of evidence, with some arguing that it points to a cover-up by the Soviet government. However, others suggest that the radiation could be explained by more mundane sources, such as thorium lantern mantles or contaminated equipment. Despite extensive analysis, the origin of the radiation remains uncertain, adding another layer of mystery to the case.

One of the more intriguing and less well-known aspects of the Dyatlov Pass incident is the claim that there was a thirteenth person involved in the expedition. According to some accounts, a mysterious figure joined the group at some point during their journey but later disappeared from the official records. This "missing thirteenth" has become a focal point for conspiracy theories, with some suggesting that this person was an agent of the KGB, sent to monitor or sabotage the group. However, there is no concrete evidence to support the existence of this thirteenth person, and most researchers believe it to be a myth. Still, the idea of an unknown figure lurking in the background adds to the aura of intrigue surrounding the case.

More than 60 years after the Dyatlov Pass incident, the mystery remains unsolved. Despite numerous investigations, documentaries, books, and even government inquiries, the true cause of the hikers' deaths has never been definitively established. The case continues to captivate people around the world, drawing in amateur sleuths, scientists, and paranormal enthusiasts alike.

In 2020, Russian authorities reopened the case, concluding that an avalanche was the most likely cause of the incident, but this explanation has done little to quell the ongoing speculation and debate. The contradictory evidence, strange injuries, and inexplicable circumstances of the hikers' deaths leave room for endless interpretation and fuel the belief that there is more to the story than meets the eye.

The Dyatlov Pass incident stands as a chilling reminder of the dangers of the wilderness, the fragility of human life, and the limits of our understanding. It is a mystery that defies easy answers, a puzzle that may never be fully solved. As long as there are questions left unanswered, the story of the nine hikers who perished in the Ural Mountains will continue to haunt those who seek the truth—a dark tale of fear, survival, and the unknown, etched into the snow-covered slopes of Dead Mountain.

Conspiracies and Cover-Ups: Fact or Fiction?
Volume 2

The Loch Ness Monster

Deep in the Scottish Highlands lies a body of water shrouded in mist and mystery: Loch Ness. Stretching over 20 miles long, a mile wide, and plunging to depths of nearly 800 feet, this dark, cold lake is the perfect setting for one of the world's most enduring legends. For centuries, tales of a creature lurking beneath the murky waters have captivated imaginations and sparked countless expeditions to uncover the truth. This creature, affectionately known as Nessie, has become the symbol of the unknown and the unexplained.

The story of the Loch Ness Monster first gained widespread attention in 1933 when George Spicer and his wife were driving along the loch's northern shore. They claimed to have seen a large, strange creature cross the road in front of them and disappear into the water. Spicer described the creature as having a long neck and a bulky body, like a dragon or prehistoric animal. His account, published in a local newspaper, set off a media frenzy, and soon, the world was abuzz with talk of the mysterious beast.

But Nessie's legend didn't start with the Spicers. In fact, stories of a monster in Loch Ness date back to ancient times. The earliest recorded sighting is found in the *Life of St. Columba,* written in the 7th century. According to this text, the Irish monk Columba encountered a water beast in the River Ness, which feeds into the loch. The creature reportedly attacked a man swimming in the river, but Columba made the sign of the cross and commanded the beast to retreat, which it did. These ancient tales, combined with the Spicers' modern account, set the stage for what would become one of the most famous cryptozoological mysteries of all time.

The Loch Ness Monster legend gained further credibility in 1934 with the release of what would become the most iconic image of Nessie: the so-called "Surgeon's Photograph." This black-and-white photo, taken by Dr. Robert Kenneth Wilson, a London gynecologist, appears to show a long-necked creature emerging from the water, its head and neck creating ripples as it moves.

The photograph was published in newspapers worldwide, capturing the public's imagination and fueling a wave of interest in the Loch Ness Monster. The image seemed to confirm what many had long suspected: that a prehistoric creature, possibly a plesiosaur—a type of long-necked marine reptile that lived during the time of the dinosaurs—was living in the depths of Loch Ness.

For decades, the Surgeon's Photograph was considered the best evidence of Nessie's existence. It inspired a series of expeditions to the loch, with scientists, adventurers, and monster hunters all eager to find definitive proof of the creature's existence. Sonar scans, underwater photography, and even submarines were employed in the search for Nessie, but the elusive monster remained frustratingly out of reach.

However, in 1994, the Surgeon's Photograph was exposed as a hoax.

Christian Spurling, the stepson of one of the men involved, confessed that the image was a carefully staged fake. The "monster" in the photograph was actually a small model, no more than a few feet long, attached to a toy submarine. The revelation shocked and disappointed many, but it did little to dampen the legend of Nessie, which had by then taken on a life of its own.

Despite the debunking of the Surgeon's Photograph, sightings of the Loch Ness Monster continued to pour in. Over the years, hundreds of people have reported seeing something unusual in the loch—strange shapes moving beneath the water, humps rising from the surface, and large disturbances in the otherwise calm waters. Some witnesses describe a creature with a long neck, while others speak of large, snake-like movements or even fins and tails breaking the surface.

In the 1960s and 1970s, the search for Nessie reached new heights, with serious scientific efforts aimed at solving the mystery once and for all. The Loch Ness Investigation Bureau, a group dedicated to studying the phenomenon, conducted long-term observations, setting up camera stations around the loch and conducting sonar scans of the depths. These efforts yielded intriguing results, including unexplained sonar readings and mysterious underwater photographs that seemed to show large, moving objects in the loch.

One of the most famous pieces of evidence from this period is the "Flipper Photo," taken by an underwater camera in 1972. The image appears to show a large, diamond-shaped flipper, which some researchers believe is consistent with the anatomy of a plesiosaur. Although the photo has been subjected to scrutiny and debate, it remains one of the more compelling pieces of evidence for Nessie's existence.

In the 21st century, the search for the Loch Ness Monster has continued, with new technologies such as drones and DNA analysis being employed to study the loch and its ecosystem. In 2018, a team of scientists conducted a comprehensive DNA survey of Loch Ness to catalog the species living in the water. While the study found no evidence of a large, unknown animal, it did detect DNA from eels, leading some to speculate that Nessie could be a giant eel rather than a prehistoric reptile. Over the years, numerous theories have been proposed to explain the Loch Ness Monster phenomenon. While some continue to believe that Nessie is a living dinosaur or a surviving plesiosaur, others have put forward more down-to-earth explanations.

One popular theory is that the sightings of Nessie are actually misidentifications of common animals or objects. Large fish, seals, otters, and even birds swimming low in the water have all been suggested as possible sources of the sightings. Natural phenomena such as waves, logs, and even optical illusions caused by the loch's unique lighting and weather conditions could also explain some of the strange sightings.

Another theory suggests that Nessie could be a type of large, unidentified aquatic animal, perhaps related to the sturgeon or catfish. These fish can grow to impressive sizes and might account for some of the more credible sightings. However, no known species matches the descriptions given by witnesses. More skeptical explanations include the idea that the Loch Ness Monster is a product of folklore and mass hysteria, with the legend growing out of ancient myths and being perpetuated by hoaxes, misidentifications, and the human tendency to see patterns where none exist.

Despite these theories, the lack of definitive evidence means that the mystery of the Loch Ness Monster remains unsolved. Nessie continues to be a symbol of the unknown, representing the enduring human fascination with the mysteries of nature and the possibility that there are still creatures lurking in the depths that we have yet to discover.

The Loch Ness Monster has transcended its origins as a local legend to become a global icon. Nessie is featured in countless books, movies, and television shows, and has inspired everything from cartoons to video games. The creature has also become a major tourist attraction, drawing visitors from around the world to the Scottish Highlands in the hope of catching a glimpse of the elusive beast.

Nessie's fame has made her a beloved figure in popular culture, often portrayed as a gentle giant or a shy, misunderstood creature. The image of Nessie has been embraced by local businesses, appearing on everything from souvenirs to whisky bottles. The legend has even inspired festivals, with the town of

Conspiracies and Cover-Ups: Fact or Fiction? Volume 2

Drumnadrochit near Loch Ness hosting an annual event celebrating all things Nessie.

But beyond the commercial aspect, the Loch Ness Monster has also had a profound impact on the field of cryptozoology—the study of unknown or hidden animals. Nessie is one of the most famous examples of a cryptid, a creature whose existence is suggested by anecdotal evidence but has yet to be confirmed by science. The search for Nessie has inspired generations of researchers, explorers, and enthusiasts to pursue their own quests for the unknown, whether it's Bigfoot, the Yeti, or other legendary creatures.

Today, the Loch Ness Monster remains one of the world's most enduring mysteries. Despite the lack of conclusive evidence, Nessie continues to captivate the imagination of people everywhere. The loch's dark, deep waters still inspire wonder, as visitors and locals alike keep watch, hoping for just one more sighting, one more ripple in the water, that might finally reveal the truth.

The legend of Nessie endures not because of proof, but because of possibility. In a world where so much has been discovered and explained, the idea that there could be something unknown lurking beneath the surface of Loch Ness is thrilling. It's a reminder that even in the 21st century, there are still mysteries that science has not solved and places where the unknown can thrive.

Whether Nessie is a prehistoric survivor, a giant eel, or merely a product of the human imagination, the Loch Ness Monster will continue to swim through the collective consciousness, a symbol of the unknown and the enduring allure of the world's mysteries. As long as there are people willing to believe, the legend of Nessie will live on, shimmering beneath the dark waters of Loch Ness, waiting for the next glimpse of the truth.

Conspiracies and Cover-Ups: Fact or Fiction? Volume 2

The Oak Island Treasure

It was the summer of 1795 when a young boy named Daniel McGinnis made a discovery on a small, uninhabited island off the coast of Nova Scotia, Canada, that would spark one of the longest and most frustrating treasure hunts in history. While exploring Oak Island, McGinnis stumbled upon a curious depression in the ground beneath a large oak tree, whose branches had been unnaturally sawed off.

Intrigued, McGinnis returned the next day with two friends, John Smith and Anthony Vaughan. They began digging into the depression, hoping to find something of value. Just a few feet down, they encountered a layer of flagstones, a sign that the hole had been deliberately covered. Excited by the prospect of treasure, the boys continued digging. At ten feet, they found a layer of oak logs, and then another layer of logs every ten feet as they dug deeper.

By the time they reached thirty feet, the boys realized they were out of their depth. They had uncovered what seemed to be a carefully engineered shaft, possibly hiding something valuable at its bottom. The mysterious construction convinced them that they were on the trail of something extraordinary—perhaps pirate treasure, or even something older and more valuable. What the boys didn't know was that they had just begun a search that would last for more than two centuries, attracting fortune seekers, engineers, and even celebrities, all of whom would be drawn to the mystery of Oak Island and its so-called "Money Pit."

News of the boys' discovery spread quickly, and before long, a group of investors formed a company called the Onslow Company to excavate the site. As they dug deeper, they encountered more layers of logs, along with clay, charcoal, and coconut fiber—an odd material, given that coconut trees do not grow anywhere near Nova Scotia.

At 90 feet, the diggers found a large stone slab inscribed with strange symbols. Though the exact translation remains debated, some claim it read, "Forty feet below, two million pounds are buried." Encouraged, the team continued digging, but their progress was suddenly halted by a disaster. The shaft, now over 100 feet deep, filled with water overnight, flooding the pit and making further excavation impossible. Attempts to pump out the water failed, and the Onslow Company eventually gave up, leaving the mysterious Money Pit and its potential riches buried beneath the island.

Over the years, numerous other expeditions were launched, each making its own discoveries. In the 1860s, one team drilled into the pit and reportedly brought up fragments of gold chain, along with a substance that resembled coconut fiber. Another expedition claimed to have struck wooden chests beneath the mud, though they were never able to retrieve them due to repeated flooding. Each time, the treasure seemed tantalizingly close, yet just out of reach. The Money Pit earned its name not because it yielded wealth, but because it swallowed it—draining the resources of every group that tried to conquer its depths.

As more people attempted to uncover Oak Island's secrets, theories about what might be hidden there grew increasingly elaborate. The most popular theory is that the pit holds pirate treasure, perhaps buried by the infamous Captain Kidd or Blackbeard. Both pirates were known to have operated in the Atlantic, and Kidd, in particular, was rumored to have buried a vast fortune before his capture.

Other theories suggest that the treasure could be even more ancient and valuable. Some believe that the pit might contain the lost treasure of the Knights Templar, the medieval order of warrior monks who were said to have hidden their vast riches after the order was disbanded in the 14th century. According to this theory, the Templars fled to the New World, bringing their treasure with them, and buried it on Oak Island for safekeeping.

Another theory posits that the Money Pit was constructed by the Spanish, who hid gold and silver looted from the Americas on the island to protect it from English pirates. Some even suggest that the pit could be the hiding place of Shakespeare's lost manuscripts, or the Ark of the Covenant. As the theories grew, so too did the mystery. How could a small island in Nova Scotia hold such secrets? The intricate design of the pit, with its layers of logs, booby traps, and flood tunnels, seemed to suggest a level of engineering far beyond what most treasure hunters would expect. Whoever built the Money Pit had gone to extraordinary lengths to protect whatever lay buried beneath it.

As the decades passed, the legend of the Oak Island treasure became intertwined with tales of a deadly curse. According to local lore, seven people must die before the treasure can be found. So far, six men have lost their lives in pursuit of the Oak Island treasure, adding a dark and ominous element to the mystery.

The first recorded death occurred in 1861 when an excavation attempt ended in tragedy. A worker died when a boiler used to pump water out of the pit exploded. Over the years, other searchers met their end through accidents and misfortunes, reinforcing the belief in the island's curse. The curse has done little to deter treasure hunters, however. If anything, it has added to the island's allure, drawing even more adventurers to its shores, all hoping to be the one to break the curse and uncover the treasure that so many had died trying to find.

In recent years, the Oak Island mystery has gained renewed attention, thanks in part to the History Channel's television series

"The Curse of Oak Island." The show follows brothers Rick and Marty Lagina, who have invested millions of dollars into the search for the treasure. Using modern technology, including sonar, ground-penetrating radar, and advanced drilling techniques, the Lagina brothers and their team have made several intriguing discoveries. They have uncovered artifacts such as old coins, human bones, and a cross that some believe could be linked to the Knights Templar.

In 2017, the team found what they believe to be a flood tunnel system designed to protect the Money Pit by channeling seawater into the shaft, further evidence of the complex engineering behind the site. Despite these discoveries, the main treasure remains elusive, continuing to evade every attempt to bring it to the surface. The show has brought Oak Island's mystery to a global audience, reigniting interest in the treasure hunt and drawing new theories and speculation. The Lagina brothers remain undeterred, convinced that they are close to solving the mystery that has baffled treasure hunters for more than two centuries.

The Oak Island mystery endures, not just because of the tantalizing possibility of buried treasure, but because of the island's ability to captivate the imagination. It is a story that combines history, adventure, and the allure of the unknown—a tale of perseverance in the face of insurmountable odds, and the relentless pursuit of a dream. Whether the treasure is real or simply a legend, the impact of Oak Island is undeniable. It has inspired books, documentaries, and countless theories, drawing people from all over the world to its shores. The story of Oak Island is a testament to the human spirit's desire to explore, discover, and uncover the secrets of the past.

As long as the Money Pit remains unsolved, Oak Island will continue to be a place of mystery and intrigue—a symbol of the eternal quest for hidden knowledge and the promise of untold riches. The search for the Oak Island treasure is not just a search for gold or jewels, but a search for answers, for understanding, and for the truth behind one of history's greatest mysteries.

Conspiracies and Cover-Ups: Fact or Fiction? Volume 2

To claim your free eBooks, visit www.LivingAmongBigfoot.com and click the FREE BOOKS tab!

Conspiracies and Cover-Ups: Fact or Fiction? Volume 2

The Ghost Ship of the Atlantic

On December 4, 1872, a British brigantine named *Dei Gratia* was sailing through the Atlantic Ocean, about 400 miles east of the Azores, when its crew spotted another ship drifting aimlessly in the distance. Captain David Morehouse, commanding the *Dei Gratia*, recognized the vessel as the *Mary Celeste*, a ship he knew well, having dined with its captain, Benjamin Briggs, just days before in New York.

The *Mary Celeste* had departed from New York on November 7, bound for Genoa, Italy, with a cargo of 1,701 barrels of denatured alcohol. On board were Captain Briggs, his wife Sarah, their two-year-old daughter Sophia, and a crew of seven experienced sailors. The voyage was expected to be routine, but as the *Dei Gratia* drew closer, it became clear that something was terribly wrong. The ship was adrift, her sails partially set but in disarray, and there was no sign of anyone on board. Concerned, Captain Morehouse sent a boarding party to investigate. What they found would baffle maritime experts and historians for over a century.

The vessel was completely abandoned. The crew's personal belongings were still in their quarters, the cargo was intact, and there was a six-month supply of food and fresh water on board. The ship's single lifeboat was missing, but there was no indication of a struggle or foul play. The *Mary Celeste* appeared eerily untouched, as if her crew had simply vanished into thin air.

The last entry in the ship's log was dated November 25, nine days before she was found. It recorded nothing unusual—just the ship's position, which was about 400 miles away from where she was discovered. The mystery of what happened to the crew of the *Mary Celeste* would go down in history as one of the greatest maritime mysteries of all time. The inexplicable disappearance of the *Mary Celeste*'s crew gave rise to a host of theories, each more intriguing than the last. Some of the most plausible explanations include natural disasters, mutiny, piracy, or foul play. However, each theory seems to leave unanswered questions.

One theory suggests that the crew abandoned ship due to the fear of an imminent explosion. The cargo of alcohol was highly flammable, and some barrels were later found to be empty. It's possible that fumes from the leaking alcohol led the crew to believe that an explosion was imminent. In a panic, they may have launched the lifeboat, intending to return once the danger had passed. But if this was the case, what happened to them afterward? Why did they never return to the ship? The lifeboat was never found, and no trace of the crew was ever discovered.

Another theory posits that the ship was caught in a sudden storm or waterspout, causing the crew to abandon ship temporarily. The *Mary Celeste* could have been pushed off course, leaving the lifeboat behind in the vast Atlantic. However, when the ship was found, it was in relatively good condition, with no signs of having been through a severe storm.

Piracy has also been suggested as a possible explanation. However, there were no signs of violence or theft on board. The cargo, which would have been valuable to pirates, was untouched. Moreover, the personal effects of the crew were still on board, ruling out robbery as a motive. Mutiny is another possibility, though it's difficult to imagine a scenario in which the entire crew—including the captain's wife and young daughter—would vanish without leaving any trace of conflict. Captain Briggs was known as a fair and capable leader, making mutiny seem unlikely. Some have speculated that the crew fell victim to foul play, possibly at the hands of another ship's crew. However, this theory also lacks evidence, as no other ship was reported in the area at the time, and the *Mary Celeste* showed no signs of a struggle.

In the absence of a clear explanation, the mystery of the *Mary Celeste* has attracted a range of more fantastical theories. Some have suggested that the ship fell victim to supernatural forces—perhaps a ghostly apparition, a sea monster, or even alien abduction. These theories, while intriguing, have little basis in reality and are largely the product of speculation and imagination.

One of the more enduring supernatural explanations is that the *Mary Celeste* entered the "Bermuda Triangle," a region of the Atlantic Ocean infamous for mysterious disappearances of ships and aircraft. However, the *Mary Celeste* was found far from this area, and there is no evidence to support the idea that the Bermuda Triangle was involved.

Another supernatural theory involves the concept of "ghost ships"—vessels that are found adrift with no crew, seemingly cursed or haunted. The *Mary Celeste* has often been described as a ghost ship due to the eerie circumstances in which it was found. The lack of any clear reason for the crew's disappearance has only fueled the idea that something otherworldly was at play. While these theories are more likely to be the stuff of legends and lore, they contribute to the mystique that surrounds the *Mary Celeste*. The ship's story has been retold in books, movies, and television shows, each adding its own layer of myth to the tale.

In the weeks following the discovery of the *Mary Celeste*, an official inquiry was launched by the British Admiralty in Gibraltar. The investigation aimed to determine what had happened to the crew and whether any foul play was involved. However, despite extensive questioning of the *Dei Gratia*'s crew and a thorough examination of the

Mary Celeste, the inquiry was unable to reach a definitive conclusion.

The ship was eventually returned to her owners, and she continued to sail for many years, though she was dogged by rumors of being cursed or haunted. In 1885, the *Mary Celeste* met a sad end when she was deliberately wrecked off the coast of Haiti in an attempted insurance fraud. The ship's captain at the time, G.C. Parker, had filled the hold with a worthless cargo and then ran her aground, hoping to collect the insurance money. The fraud was quickly discovered, and Parker was arrested and disgraced. Despite the ship's ignoble end, the mystery of the *Mary Celeste* has endured. The lack of any concrete evidence or conclusive explanation has kept the story alive, making it one of the most famous unsolved maritime mysteries in history.

The story of the *Mary Celeste* has captivated people for over a century, inspiring countless books, articles, and fictionalized accounts. It has become a symbol of the unknown and the unknowable—a reminder that, even in the modern world, some mysteries remain unsolved. The subject of numerous investigations and theories, with each new generation of researchers attempting to crack the case. Yet, despite advances in forensic science, maritime archaeology, and historical research, the fate of the ship's crew remains a mystery. Theories come and go, but none have provided a definitive answer to what happened on that fateful voyage in 1872.

In many ways, the *Mary Celeste* is more than just a story about a lost crew; it is a tale that speaks to our deepest fears and curiosities. The idea that a ship could be found adrift, her crew vanished without a trace, taps into the human fascination with the sea and the unknown. The story has become a metaphor for the mysteries of life itself—unpredictable, sometimes inexplicable, and forever compelling.

The legend has also contributed to the broader mythology of the sea, where ghost ships, cursed vessels, and supernatural occurrences are common themes. It is a story that has transcended its historical roots to become part of the collective imagination, a tale that will likely continue to be told for generations to come.

Today, the *Mary Celeste* remains one of the greatest maritime mysteries of all time. Despite countless theories and investigations, the true fate of Captain Briggs, his family, and his crew has never been determined. The ship's story endures as a cautionary tale about the dangers of the sea and the limits of human knowledge.

Conspiracies and Cover-Ups: Fact or Fiction? Volume 2

As with many great mysteries, the allure of the *Mary Celeste* lies in its unresolved nature. The absence of a clear answer invites endless speculation and debate, ensuring that the story remains fresh in the minds of those who hear it. Whether the crew's disappearance was the result of a natural disaster, human error, or something more sinister, the *Mary Celeste* continues to sail through the annals of history as a ghost ship—forever adrift, her secrets locked away in the deep, dark waters of the Atlantic.

In the end, the mystery of the *Mary Celeste* is not just about what happened to her crew, but about the broader human desire to explore, discover, and understand the unknown. It is a reminder that, even in a world where science and technology have unlocked many of nature's secrets, there are still some mysteries that defy explanation, leaving us to wonder and imagine what might have been.

Conspiracies and Cover-Ups: Fact or Fiction?
Volume 2

The Tunguska Event

It was a clear morning on June 30, 1908, in the remote Siberian wilderness near the Tunguska River. The region, covered with dense forest and inhabited only by a few reindeer herders and nomadic Evenki people, was just beginning to wake up. The peaceful stillness of the morning was suddenly shattered by a blinding flash of light in the sky, followed by a deafening explosion that could be heard for hundreds of miles.

The explosion was so powerful that it flattened an estimated 80 million trees over an area of 830 square miles, creating a blast zone that stretched as far as the eye could see. The shockwave from the blast was felt as far away as Western Europe, and seismographs in places as distant as Washington, D.C., recorded the event.

Witnesses who were close enough to see the event described a massive fireball streaking across the sky, followed by a series of loud booms and a shockwave that knocked them off their feet. The sky reportedly glowed for several nights afterward, and strange atmospheric phenomena were observed across Europe and Asia. Despite the magnitude of the explosion, it left behind no crater, no obvious impact site. The Tunguska Event, as it would come to be known, was a mystery from the start, and it would take decades for scientists to begin to piece together what might have caused one of the most powerful explosions in recorded history.

In the years immediately following the Tunguska Event, Russia was in political and social turmoil, and it wasn't until 1927—nearly 20 years later—that the first scientific expedition was organized to investigate the site. Led by Russian mineralogist Leonid Kulik, the team ventured into the remote Siberian taiga, a journey fraught with difficulties due to the region's harsh conditions and lack of infrastructure.

When Kulik and his team finally arrived at the epicenter of the explosion, they were astonished by what they found. The forest was devastated, with trees lying flat on the ground, all pointing away from the center of the blast like the spokes of a giant wheel. In the middle of this destruction stood a small number of scorched and charred trees, still upright, their branches stripped bare by the blast. The scene was eerie, like the aftermath of an apocalyptic event.

However, what Kulik didn't find was just as perplexing as what he did. Despite the immense power of the explosion, there was no sign of a crater, no obvious impact site, and no traces of the object that had caused the destruction. Kulik hypothesized that the event was caused by the impact of a large meteorite, which had exploded above the ground, causing the devastation below. But without any fragments of the meteorite to examine, his theory remained unproven. Kulik led several more expeditions to the area over the following years, but each time, the results were the same—no conclusive evidence of what had caused the Tunguska Event. The mystery deepened, and speculation about what had happened on that fateful morning in 1908 began to grow.

Over the years, a wide range of theories has been proposed to explain the Tunguska Event. The most widely accepted scientific explanation is that it was caused by the airburst of a small asteroid or comet entering Earth's atmosphere. This object, estimated to be about 200 feet in diameter, would have heated up rapidly as it descended, creating a massive explosion as it disintegrated in the atmosphere, releasing energy equivalent to 10-15 megatons of TNT—about 1,000 times more powerful than the atomic bomb dropped on Hiroshima.

This theory explains the lack of an impact crater, as the explosion occurred several miles above the ground, and it accounts for the widespread devastation and the absence of large meteorite fragments. The idea of a comet is also supported by the fact that no metallic debris was found, suggesting that the object may have been made primarily of ice, which would have vaporized upon entering the atmosphere. However, not everyone is satisfied with this explanation, and alternative theories have been put forward over the years. Some of these are more plausible than others, but all reflect the enduring mystery of the event.

One alternative theory suggests that the explosion was caused by a natural gas explosion from below the Earth's surface, where methane released from the permafrost could have ignited, creating a massive underground explosion. This theory, while intriguing, struggles to explain the eyewitness reports of a fireball in the sky or the specific pattern of tree destruction. Another theory posits that the event was caused by a small black hole passing through the Earth, but this hypothesis is considered highly speculative and lacks supporting evidence. A similar idea involves a burst of antimatter colliding with Earth, but this too remains in the realm of science fiction rather than science fact.

Perhaps the most outlandish theory is that the Tunguska Event was the result of an alien spacecraft crash or some form of advanced weaponry being tested, possibly by Nikola Tesla, who was experimenting with wireless energy transmission at the time. While these ideas capture the imagination, they are not supported by any credible evidence and are generally dismissed by the scientific community.

The Tunguska Event has had a profound impact not only on the scientific community but also on popular culture. It has inspired countless books, films, and television shows, often portraying the event as a key moment in a larger narrative about extraterrestrial life, secret weapons, or unexplained phenomena. The mystery of what happened in the remote Siberian wilderness has captured the imagination of people around the world, becoming a symbol of the unknown and the potential for catastrophic events that are beyond our control.

For scientists, the Tunguska Event has served as a stark reminder of the dangers posed by near-Earth objects (NEOs)—asteroids and comets that could potentially collide with our planet. It has spurred ongoing research into the detection and tracking of NEOs, as well as efforts to develop strategies for mitigating the threat they pose.

In 1991, the U.S. Congress mandated that NASA identify and track all NEOs larger than one kilometer in diameter—objects that could cause global devastation if they were to collide with Earth. This effort, known as the Spaceguard program, has since expanded to include the tracking of smaller objects as well, recognizing that even much smaller impacts, like the one believed to have caused the Tunguska Event, could result in significant regional damage. The event has also led to a greater understanding of the dynamics of atmospheric explosions and the effects of impact events on Earth. Studies of the blast pattern at Tunguska have provided valuable insights into how such events could unfold, informing models used to predict the potential impact of future airbursts or impacts.

In recent years, advances in technology and scientific methods have led to new insights into the Tunguska Event, although the core mystery remains unsolved. Satellite imagery, computer simulations, and analysis of tree rings and soil samples have all contributed to a better understanding of what might have happened.

In 2007, Italian researchers from the University of Bologna proposed that Lake Cheko, a small lake located near the epicenter of the explosion, might be an impact crater created by a fragment of the Tunguska object. The team suggested that a piece of the object survived the initial explosion and struck the ground, forming the lake. However, subsequent studies have questioned this theory, arguing that the lake is likely much older than the event itself.

Other researchers have revisited the comet hypothesis, examining the chemical composition of soil samples from the Tunguska region for traces of extraterrestrial material. While some studies have reported finding unusual isotopic ratios that could be indicative of a cometary origin, these findings remain controversial and have yet to be definitively confirmed.

Despite these efforts, the Tunguska Event remains an open

question. While the asteroid or comet hypothesis is the most widely accepted explanation, the lack of direct evidence—such as fragments of the impactor—means that the debate is likely to continue for years to come. The subject stands as one of the greatest scientific mysteries of the modern era—a reminder of the unpredictable and sometimes violent forces that exist within our universe. The remote Siberian forest, with its flattened trees and eerie silence, serves as a testament to the power of an explosion that shook the world without warning.

As humanity continues to explore the cosmos, the Tunguska Event is a sobering example of the potential dangers that lie beyond our atmosphere. It underscores the importance of understanding and preparing for the possibility of future impacts, even as it invites us to ponder the mysteries of our planet and the universe. More than a century after the event, the Tunguska explosion remains an enduring mystery, a puzzle that has yet to be fully solved. It is a story that captivates scientists and laypeople alike, a tale of devastation, mystery, and the limits of human knowledge.

Whether we will ever uncover the full truth of what happened that morning in 1908 is uncertain. But as long as there are questions to be asked and mysteries to be explored, the

Tunguska Event will continue to fascinate and inspire, reminding us of the vast and sometimes unknowable forces that shape our world.

Visit My Digital Book Store

If you're looking for NEW reads, check out my digital store, www.TomLyonsBooks.com.

Buying my books directly from me means you save money—because my store will always sell for less than big retailers. My store also offers sales, deals, bundles, and pre-order discounts you won't find anywhere else.

Visit my store now to get a FREE audiobook!

Conspiracies and Cover-Ups: Fact or Fiction? Volume 2

The Lost Colony

In the late 16th century, England was eager to establish a permanent foothold in the New World. Queen Elizabeth I granted Sir Walter Raleigh a charter to explore and colonize land in North America. After an initial failed attempt in 1585, Raleigh sent another group of settlers in 1587, led by John White, to establish a colony on Roanoke Island, located off the coast of present-day North Carolina.

The settlers, numbering around 115 men, women, and children, arrived in July 1587 and quickly set about building their new home. Among them was White's daughter, Eleanor Dare, who gave birth to Virginia Dare, the first English child born in the New World. Spirits were high despite the challenges they faced, and the settlers hoped to create a prosperous colony that would be a beacon of English culture in the New World.

However, the colony soon ran into difficulties. Food supplies dwindled, relations with the local Native American tribes were strained, and the settlers became increasingly isolated. In late 1587, the colonists convinced John White to return to England to seek help and additional supplies. White reluctantly agreed, leaving behind his family and fellow settlers with a promise to return as quickly as possible.

But White's return to Roanoke was delayed by the outbreak of the Anglo-Spanish War, which tied up England's ships and resources. It would be nearly three years before White could return to the island. When he finally did, in August 1590, what he found—or rather, what he didn't find—would spark one of the greatest mysteries in American history.

Conspiracies and Cover-Ups: Fact or Fiction? Volume 2

When John White's ship arrived at Roanoke Island in 1590, the sight that greeted him was one of desolation. The settlement, which he had left thriving, was eerily deserted. The houses and fortifications were still standing, but they had been dismantled and stripped of anything useful. There was no sign of a struggle or any indication that the settlers had left in haste. It was as if they had simply vanished.

White's search of the area revealed only a few cryptic clues. Carved into a post of the fort was the word "CROATOAN," and nearby, another tree bore the letters "CRO." The significance of these carvings was unclear, but White took them as a possible indication that the settlers had moved to Croatoan Island (now known as Hatteras Island), some 50 miles to the south. However, bad weather and other factors prevented White from searching the island, and he was forced to return to England without discovering the fate of his colony.

The disappearance of the Roanoke settlers remains one of history's greatest unsolved mysteries. No definitive evidence has ever been found to explain what happened to them, and their fate has been the subject of endless speculation and debate. Did they assimilate with local Native American tribes? Were they killed by hostile forces? Or did they attempt to move elsewhere, only to meet an unknown fate? The possibilities are numerous, but the answers remain elusive.

Over the centuries, many theories have been proposed to explain the disappearance of the Roanoke settlers. Each theory offers a different interpretation of the sparse evidence left behind and reflects the various challenges that the colony faced in its early days.

One of the most widely accepted theories is that the colonists sought refuge with the Croatoan tribe, who were known to be friendly toward the English. This theory is supported by the carvings left behind and by accounts from later settlers who reported seeing European-looking individuals among the Native American tribes in the region. According to this theory, the settlers may have assimilated into the tribe, adopting their customs and way of life to survive in the harsh conditions of the New World.

Another theory suggests that the colonists attempted to relocate to the Chesapeake Bay area, where they had originally intended to settle before being diverted to Roanoke. Proponents of this theory argue that the settlers may have built new homes in the Chesapeake region but were later attacked and killed by hostile Native American tribes or Spanish forces.

However, no conclusive evidence has been found to support this idea.

A grimmer theory posits that the settlers perished from disease, starvation, or exposure. The region was known for its harsh climate and difficult living conditions, and it's possible that the colonists simply could not survive without additional supplies and assistance. In this scenario, the survivors may have tried to move inland or to other locations, leaving behind the carvings as a message for any rescuers who might come looking for them.

Some researchers have even speculated that the colonists were victims of a Spanish attack. At the time, Spain was England's chief rival, and the Spanish were actively patrolling the Atlantic coast to protect their own interests. It's possible that a Spanish force discovered the Roanoke colony and destroyed it, although no records exist to confirm this.

The "lost colony" has also been linked to more fantastical explanations, including supernatural events and curses. These theories, while popular in folklore, lack any historical basis and are generally dismissed by historians.

The search for evidence of what happened to the Roanoke settlers has continued for more than four centuries, with historians, archaeologists, and amateur sleuths all attempting to solve the mystery.

Over the years, several archaeological digs have been conducted on Roanoke Island, Croatoan Island, and other nearby locations in the hope of uncovering clues.

In the early 1990s, archaeologists discovered English artifacts on Hatteras Island (formerly Croatoan Island), including a musket barrel and a silver ring that appeared to date back to the late 16th century. These findings suggest that at least some of the settlers may have lived on the island for a time. However, the evidence is not conclusive, and it remains unclear whether these artifacts belonged to the original Roanoke colonists or to later settlers.

In 2012, researchers announced the discovery of a hidden symbol on an old map known as the "Virginia Pars" map, which was created by John White himself. The symbol, covered by a patch on the map, seemed to indicate a fort or settlement in the interior of North Carolina. This led to new excavations in the area, where archaeologists uncovered English pottery and other artifacts that could be linked to the Roanoke settlers. Yet, while these discoveries are intriguing, they have not definitively answered the question of what happened to the colony.

Despite these efforts, the exact fate of the Roanoke settlers remains a mystery. The lack of concrete evidence has allowed speculation to flourish, and the story of the "lost colony" continues to captivate the imagination.

The mystery of the Roanoke colony has become a defining legend in American history, symbolizing the challenges and uncertainties faced by early settlers in the New World. The tale of the "lost colony" has been retold countless times in books, films, and television shows, each adding its own interpretation to the story.

Virginia Dare, the first English child born in America, has become a particularly enduring figure in American folklore. Her name is associated with numerous places, institutions, and even commercial products, reflecting the lasting legacy of the Roanoke colony. The mystery of what happened to Virginia and her fellow colonists has become a metaphor for the unknown dangers of the frontier and the enduring spirit of exploration.

The story of Roanoke has also served as a cautionary tale, reminding later generations of the difficulties faced by those who sought to establish a new life in an unfamiliar and often hostile land. The disappearance of the Roanoke settlers underscores the fragility of early colonial ventures and the importance of preparation, resources, and cooperation with indigenous peoples.

In modern times, the Roanoke mystery has inspired numerous fictional works, from novels and plays to horror films and television series. The idea of a vanished colony, leaving behind only cryptic clues and unanswered questions, continues to resonate with audiences, symbolizing the eternal human quest for discovery and understanding.

More than 400 years after the disappearance of the Roanoke settlers, the mystery remains unsolved. Despite extensive research, archaeological discoveries, and countless theories, no definitive answer has been found. The fate of the "lost colony" continues to be one of the most enduring mysteries in American history.

As new technologies and methods of investigation are developed, there is always hope that the mystery of Roanoke may one day be solved. But even if the truth is never fully uncovered, the story of the lost colony will continue to captivate the imagination, serving as a reminder of the challenges faced by early settlers and the enduring allure of the unknown.

The Roanoke colony is more than just a historical puzzle; it is a symbol of the human spirit's resilience in the face of adversity and the mysteries that still lie hidden in the shadows of history. The carvings of

"CROATOAN" and "CRO" on the trees remain as the only tangible clues, mysterious markers of a story that has fascinated generations and will likely continue to do so for generations to come.

In the end, the lost colony of Roanoke represents the intersection of history and legend, a place where fact and fiction merge to create a tale that is both haunting and inspiring. As long as there are mysteries to be explored and stories to be told, the fate of the Roanoke settlers will remain one of the most compelling chapters in the saga of the New World.

The Phoenix Lights

On the evening of March 13, 1997, the skies over Phoenix, Arizona, became the stage for one of the most widely witnessed and puzzling UFO events in modern history. Known as the "Phoenix Lights," this mysterious incident would go on to captivate the imaginations of people across the world and spark a debate that continues to this day.

The phenomenon began shortly after sunset, when a series of lights appeared in the sky over the town of Henderson, Nevada. Witnesses described seeing a V-shaped formation of five to seven lights moving silently across the sky. The lights were bright, and they seemed to hover in perfect formation. They were unlike any aircraft or natural phenomenon that the witnesses had seen before.

As the evening progressed, the lights continued on a southeasterly course, passing over the cities of Paulden, Prescott, and Dewey before reaching Phoenix around 8:30 PM. By this time, hundreds, if not thousands, of people had witnessed the phenomenon, and reports were flooding in to local radio stations, news outlets, and even the police.

In Phoenix, the lights were seen by people from all walks of life—residents, tourists, and even the state governor. Witnesses described a massive, dark triangular or V-shaped object that seemed to block out the stars as it passed overhead. The object moved slowly and silently, gliding across the sky at an altitude estimated to be between 1,000 and 2,000 feet. Some reported that the lights changed color as they moved, while others said they saw smaller lights trailing behind the main formation.

Despite the scale of the event and the number of witnesses, no one could explain what they were seeing. There were no official reports of military exercises or aircraft in the area, and the lights did not behave like any known aircraft or natural phenomenon. As the night wore on, the lights gradually disappeared, leaving behind a city full of people who were stunned, confused, and eager for answers.

The Phoenix Lights quickly became the talk of the town, with local media outlets covering the story extensively. The sheer number of witnesses and the consistency of their reports made it clear that something unusual had happened. But what exactly that "something" was remained a mystery.

In the days and weeks that followed, the story spread beyond Phoenix, attracting national and even international attention. UFO enthusiasts and researchers flocked to Arizona, eager to interview witnesses and gather as much information as possible. The event was quickly labeled one of the most significant UFO sightings in history, and theories about the nature of the lights began to emerge.

Some witnesses believed that they had seen a secret military aircraft, perhaps an experimental stealth bomber or reconnaissance plane. Others speculated that the lights were part of a large-scale military exercise or a formation of flares dropped by aircraft. But these explanations failed to account for the size, shape, and behavior of the object described by so many witnesses.

For many, the most compelling explanation was that the lights were evidence of an extraterrestrial spacecraft. The idea that a massive UFO could fly over a major American city without detection or explanation captured the public's imagination and led to a renewed interest in the possibility of alien life. UFO organizations and researchers began to investigate the incident in earnest, collecting testimonies, analyzing video footage, and attempting to piece together what had happened.

The incident also caught the attention of skeptics and debunkers, who argued that the lights were most likely a misidentification of conventional aircraft, flares, or even a hoax. The lack of concrete evidence and the absence of radar data to support the UFO theory led many to dismiss the event as a case of mass hysteria or misperception.

But for those who had witnessed the lights firsthand, the experience was profound and unsettling. Many described a sense of awe and fear as they watched the silent, dark object pass overhead. The Phoenix Lights had left an indelible mark on the community, and the question of what had really happened that night remained unanswered.

In the immediate aftermath of the Phoenix Lights, the U.S. government and military were conspicuously silent. Despite the widespread public interest and the numerous eyewitness reports, there was no official statement or explanation offered by the authorities. This silence only fueled speculation and suspicion, leading many to believe that the government was hiding something.

It wasn't until several months later that the military finally offered an explanation. According to the official story, the lights seen over

Phoenix were flares dropped by A-10 Warthog aircraft during a routine training exercise at the Barry M. Goldwater Range, a military testing area southwest of the city. The flares, which are used to illuminate targets on the ground, were said to have been released in a pattern that could have created the appearance of a large, V-shaped object.

However, this explanation was met with skepticism by many who had witnessed the event. The flares theory did not account for the size, shape, or behavior of the object described by witnesses, nor did it explain why the lights were seen moving steadily across the sky for such a long distance. Additionally, no evidence was provided to support the claim that a flare drop had occurred at the time of the sighting.

The government's explanation did little to quell the controversy, and it only added to the perception that something was being covered up. The lack of transparency and the delay in providing an explanation led many to believe that the Phoenix Lights were part of a secret military project or even evidence of extraterrestrial visitation.

Even Arizona's governor at the time, Fife Symington, weighed in on the incident. Initially, Symington made light of the event, holding a press conference in which he jokingly presented a staff member dressed as an alien. But years later, Symington revealed that he had actually witnessed the lights himself and believed that they were not of this world. His admission added a new layer of intrigue to the mystery and reignited public interest in the case.

The Phoenix Lights incident has given rise to a wide range of theories, each attempting to explain what happened that night. While the official explanation of flares remains the government's stance, other theories have gained traction over the years. One popular theory is that the lights were part of a secret military experiment or test involving advanced aircraft or technology. Proponents of this theory point to the shape and behavior of the object, which seemed to defy conventional aerodynamics. They suggest that the government may have been testing a new type of aircraft, possibly a stealth or anti-gravity vehicle, and that the lights were the result of this secret technology.

Another theory is that the lights were a mass sighting of an extraterrestrial spacecraft. Many witnesses reported seeing a large, solid object that blocked out the stars as it moved overhead, leading to speculation that it was a "mother ship" or alien craft visiting Earth. This theory is supported by the fact that similar sightings of V-shaped or triangular UFOs have been reported around the world, leading some to believe that such objects are part of a larger pattern of alien activity.

Skeptics, on the other hand, argue that the lights were simply misidentified conventional aircraft or a case of mass hysteria. They point out that the lights could have been the result of ordinary aircraft flying in formation, and that the unusual conditions of the night—such as atmospheric distortion or optical illusions—may have caused witnesses to misinterpret what they were seeing.

Another skeptical explanation is that the event was a combination of different phenomena: the V-shaped lights seen earlier in the evening could have been aircraft, while the lights seen later could have been flares. This theory suggests that the two incidents were unrelated but were conflated in the minds of witnesses and the public.

The Phoenix Lights incident has had a lasting impact on both the UFO community and popular culture. It is often cited as one of the most credible and well-documented UFO sightings in history, thanks to the sheer number of witnesses and the consistency of their reports. The event has been the subject of numerous documentaries, books, and television programs, and it continues to be a focal point for UFO researchers and enthusiasts.

In addition to its influence on UFO studies, the Phoenix Lights have also become a cultural touchstone, symbolizing the enduring human fascination with the unknown. The incident has inspired works of fiction, including movies, novels, and even video games, and it has contributed to the broader narrative of extraterrestrial life and government secrecy.

The incident has also had a profound effect on the witnesses themselves. Many of those who saw the lights have reported a lasting sense of wonder and curiosity, and some have become outspoken advocates for greater transparency and investigation into the phenomenon. For them, the Phoenix Lights are not just an unsolved mystery, but a deeply personal experience that has reshaped their understanding of the world.

More than two decades after the Phoenix Lights lit up the night sky, the incident remains an enduring mystery. Despite the official explanations and the various theories that have been proposed, no one has been able to definitively explain what happened on March 13, 1997. The event continues to be a source of fascination and debate, with new information and perspectives emerging over time.

In recent years, the Phoenix Lights have become a symbol of the broader UFO phenomenon, representing the tension between official narratives and the experiences of ordinary people. The incident raises important questions about the limits of our knowledge, the role of government in controlling information, and the possibility that we are not alone in the universe.

As long as these questions remain unanswered, the Phoenix Lights will continue to captivate the imagination and inspire those who seek to uncover the truth. Whether the lights were the result of advanced technology, extraterrestrial visitation, or something else entirely, they serve as a reminder that there are still mysteries in our world that defy easy explanation.

The night the sky went dark over Phoenix will likely remain one of the most intriguing and unexplained events in modern history—a moment when thousands of people looked up and saw something extraordinary, something that challenges our understanding of reality and our place in the cosmos. The Phoenix Lights are a testament to the power of the unknown, and their legacy will endure as long as we continue to search for answers.

Conspiracies and Cover-Ups: Fact or Fiction?
Volume 2

Conclusion

Thanks for reading! If you want more, read *Conspiracies and Cover-Ups, Volume 3*.

Conspiracies and Cover-Ups: Fact or Fiction?
Volume 2

Conspiracies and Cover-Ups: Fact or Fiction? Volume 2

Editor's Note

Before you go, I'd like to say "thank you" for purchasing this book.

I know you had various cryptid-related books to choose from, but you took a chance at my content.
Therefore, thanks for reading this one and sticking with it to the last page.

At this point, I'd like to ask you for a *tiny* favor; it would mean the world if you could leave a review wherever you purchased this book.

Your feedback will aid me in creating products you and many others can enjoy.

Conspiracies and Cover-Ups: Fact or Fiction?
Volume 2

Conspiracies and Cover-Ups: Fact or Fiction? Volume 2

Mailing List Sign-Up Form

Don't forget to sign up for the newsletter email list. I promise I will not use it to spam you but to ensure you always receive the first word on any new releases, discounts, or giveaways! You only need to visit the following URL and enter your email address.

URL-

http://eepurl.com/dhnspT

Social Media

Feel free to follow/reach out to me with questions or concerns on either Instagram or Twitter! I will do my best to follow back and respond to all comments.

Instagram:

@living_among_bigfoot

Twitter:

@AmongBigfoot

Conspiracies and Cover-Ups: Fact or Fiction?
Volume 2

About the Editor

A simple man at heart, Tom Lyons lived an ordinary existence for his first 52 years. Native to the great state of Wisconsin, he went through the motions of everyday life, residing near his family and developing a successful online business. The world he once knew would completely change shortly after moving out west, where he was confronted by the allegedly mythical species known as Bigfoot.

You can email him directly at:

Living.Among.Bigfoot@gmail.com

Printed in Great Britain
by Amazon